TAYLOR SWIFT

Drop Everything Now

Daniel D. Lee
A SkyCuration
★★★★★

I. Introduction
    A. A brief overview of Taylor Swift's career
    B. Importance of Taylor Swift as a pop icon
    C. Significance of her journey in the music industry
II. Early Life and Beginnings
    A. Childhood and family background
    B. Introduction to music and early influences
    C. Pursuit of a career in the music industry
    D. Challenges faced in her initial years
III. Breaking Through: The Start of Taylor Swift's Career
    A. The release of her debut album "Taylor Swift"

B. The success of singles like "Tim McGraw" and "Teardrops on My Guitar"

C. Establishing herself as a country music sensation

IV. Crossover Success and Rise to Superstardom

A. The release of "Fearless" and its massive success

B. Transition from country to pop music

C. Unprecedented achievements and accolades

V. Redefining Pop Music

A. The release of "1989" and its impact on the pop music scene

B. Creation of memorable music videos and live performances

C. Embracing her role as a pop music icon

VI. The Art of Songwriting

A. Taylor Swift's approach to songwriting

B. The stories behind some of her biggest hits

C. Her evolution as a songwriter over the years

VII. Personal Life and Relationships

A. Romantic relationships and the media's scrutiny

B. Friendship with other celebrities and the creation of her "squad"

C. Balancing fame, privacy, and personal growth

VIII. Overcoming Adversity

A. Struggles with media portrayal and public opinion

B. The feud with Kanye West and Kim Kardashian

C. The release of "Reputation" and its portrayal of her experiences

IX. Philanthropy and Activism

A. Support for charitable organizations and causes

B. Advocacy for women's rights and gender equality

C. Political involvement and public stance on various issues

D. Influence on fans and using her platform for good

X. The "Taylor's Version" Era

A. The decision to re-record her old albums

B. The impact and reception of "Taylor's Version" albums

C. The significance of this move in the music industry

XI. The Power of Fandom: Swifties

A. The formation and growth of her fanbase

B. Her relationship with her fans

C. The role of her fans in her success

XII. Taylor Swift and the Media

A. Her relationship with the media over the years

B. The impact of media scrutiny on her life and career

C. Her strategies for managing her public image

XIII. Taylor Swift's Impact on Social Media

A. Her use of social media platforms

B. The influence of her social media presence

C. Her engagement with fans on social media

XIV. The Evolution of Taylor Swift

A. The release of "Lover" and embracing a more positive outlook

B. Exploring different genres and artistic styles

C. The role of personal growth and self-discovery in her journey

XVI. Legacy and Impact

A. Taylor Swift's influence on the music industry

B. The lasting effect on pop culture and future generations

C. Nurturing new talent and paying it forward

D. Taylor Swift as a symbol of perseverance and resilience

XVII. Ventures Beyond Music

A. Acting career and guest appearances in TV and film

B. Collaborations with other artists and songwriting for others

C. Entrepreneurial pursuits, including her fashion line and fragrance collection

XVIII. Taylor Swift's Influence on Aspiring Musicians

A. The impact of her journey on aspiring artists

B. Tips and advice from Taylor Swift for those pursuing a career in music

C. Examples of successful artists influenced by her work

D. The importance of mentorship and support in the music

industry
XIX. The Future of Taylor Swift
   A. Her plans for future music and tours
   B. Potential new directions in her career
   C. Her aspirations outside of music
XX. Conclusion
   A. The importance of Taylor Swift's journey as an inspiration to others
   B. The power of self-belief and perseverance in achieving success
   C. Taylor Swift's enduring success and her lasting impact on the world

I. INTRODUCTION

A. A brief overview of Taylor Swift's career

T aylor Swift, an American singer-songwriter, has experienced a meteoric rise to fame since she first entered the music industry. Born on December 13, 1989, in Reading, Pennsylvania, Swift has become one of the most successful and influential artists of her generation. Her career began with her self-titled debut album in 2006, which introduced her as a young country music sensation. With a penchant for heartfelt, narrative-driven songs, Swift soon captivated audiences worldwide.

Over the years, she has successfully transitioned from country to pop music, consistently breaking records and earning numerous accolades along the way. Albums like "Fearless," "1989," "Reputation," and "Lover" have showcased her ability to reinvent her sound while maintaining her signature storytelling style. Her music videos and live performances have further cemented her status as a pop icon.

In addition to her musical achievements, Swift has also ventured into acting, entrepreneurship, and philanthropy. She has used her platform to advocate for women's rights, gender equality, and other important social issues. As a mentor and inspiration for aspiring musicians, Swift's career exemplifies the power of self-belief, perseverance, and resilience in achieving success.

B. Importance of Taylor Swift as a pop icon

Taylor Swift has become one of the most influential and important pop icons of her generation. Since her debut in the music scene, she has consistently pushed boundaries and redefined the landscape of pop music. As an artist, songwriter, and performer, Taylor Swift has played an integral role in shaping the industry, influencing both her contemporaries and future generations of musicians.

One of the key factors that contribute to Swift's importance as a pop icon is her ability to constantly reinvent herself and her music. From her roots in country music to her transition into pop, she has demonstrated remarkable versatility and an innate ability to adapt to different genres. By doing so, Swift has managed to maintain her relevance and appeal to a wide range of audiences.

Another aspect of Swift's importance as a pop icon is her commitment to authenticity and storytelling. Her deeply personal and relatable lyrics have resonated with millions of fans worldwide, allowing them to connect with her music on a profound level. Through her songs, Swift has been able to share her experiences and emotions, creating a bond with her audience that transcends the typical artist-fan relationship.

Taylor Swift is also renowned for her powerful live performances and visually striking music videos. These elements have become a key component of her pop icon status, showcasing her exceptional talent and creativity. As an influential figure in pop culture, Swift has managed to shape trends and redefine the standards of modern-day entertainment.

In addition to her music career, Swift's importance as a pop icon extends to her activism and philanthropy. She has used her platform to raise awareness and contribute to numerous charitable organizations and causes, advocating for women's rights, gender equality, and social justice. Through her actions, she has inspired countless fans to follow in her footsteps and make a difference in the world.

Finally, Taylor Swift's perseverance and resilience in the face of adversity have solidified her importance as a pop icon. She has faced various challenges throughout her career, including public feuds, media scrutiny, and personal struggles. Yet, she has always managed to overcome these obstacles and continue to thrive in the industry.

In conclusion, Taylor Swift's importance as a pop icon lies in her ability to constantly evolve, her commitment to authenticity, her impressive performances, her dedication to activism, and her resilience in the face of adversity. As a symbol of perseverance and self-belief, she has inspired millions of fans around the world and has left an indelible mark on the music industry and pop culture.

C. Significance of her journey in the music industry

Taylor Swift's journey in the music industry has been marked by continuous evolution, breaking boundaries, and overcoming adversity. Her career serves as an important example for aspiring artists and fans alike, highlighting the significance of passion, hard work, and resilience in achieving success.

Swift's transition from country to pop music showcases her versatility as an artist and her ability to adapt to the ever-changing landscape of the music industry. Her consistent reinvention and growth, both as a musician and as a person, have allowed her to remain relevant and influential throughout her career. By embracing different genres, styles, and artistic approaches, Swift has demonstrated the importance of creativity and innovation in the music world.

Furthermore, her journey has been characterized by a fearless approach to addressing personal experiences and emotions in her music. By candidly sharing her life through her lyrics, Swift has resonated with millions of fans and created a deep, personal connection with her audience. This authenticity has set her apart from many other artists and has contributed significantly to her success.

Swift has also faced numerous challenges and controversies throughout her career, such as public feuds, media scrutiny, and battles for creative control. By overcoming these adversities, she has emerged as a symbol of perseverance and resilience, inspiring others to stand up for themselves and pursue their dreams despite obstacles.

Lastly, her journey in the music industry has been marked by a commitment to philanthropy and activism. Swift has used her platform to raise awareness and advocate for various social issues, demonstrating the power and responsibility that comes with fame. This aspect of her career serves as an important reminder that success goes beyond personal achievements and includes making a positive impact on the world.

In summary, Taylor Swift's journey in the music industry is significant for its demonstration of artistic evolution, resilience, authenticity, and the importance of using one's platform for good.

II. EARLY LIFE AND BEGINNINGS

A. Childhood and family background

Taylor Alison Swift was born on December 13, 1989, in Reading, Pennsylvania. She is the daughter of Scott Kingsley Swift, a financial advisor, and Andrea Gardner Swift, a former marketing executive and homemaker. Taylor has one younger brother, Austin Swift, who pursued a career in acting. Her family background played a significant role in shaping her passion for music and her career aspirations.

Swift's ancestry is primarily German, English, Scottish, and Irish. She was named after the American singer-songwriter James Taylor, which would later prove to be a fitting tribute to her own career in music. Growing up, Taylor was surrounded by a variety of musical influences, thanks to her parents' diverse taste in music. This exposure laid the foundation for her love and appreciation for different genres.

As a child, Swift showed a keen interest in performing arts. She often participated in local theater productions, and her parents encouraged her to explore her talents. Recognizing her potential, they enrolled her in vocal and acting lessons to help her hone her skills.

When Taylor was nine years old, her family moved to a rural area in Wyomissing, Pennsylvania. It was during this time that she was first introduced to country music, which would eventually become a defining aspect of her early career. Inspired by artists like Shania Twain, Faith Hill, and the Dixie Chicks, Taylor began to develop her own unique style and identity as a singer-songwriter.

Swift's parents were incredibly supportive of her dreams, often driving her to performances, auditions, and industry events.

Recognizing the need for their daughter to be closer to the music industry, the Swift family made a life-changing decision to move to Nashville, Tennessee, when Taylor was just 14 years old. This move would prove to be the catalyst for her successful career in the music industry.

In conclusion, Taylor Swift's childhood and family background played a crucial role in shaping her passion for music and her determination to succeed. Her early exposure to diverse musical influences, combined with her family's unwavering support, laid the groundwork for her rise to superstardom as a singer-songwriter and pop icon.

B. Introduction to music
and early influences

From a young age, Taylor Swift displayed a natural affinity for music. Growing up in a supportive and creative household, she was introduced to various musical genres by her parents, who themselves had a deep appreciation for music. Her mother, Andrea Swift, was a marketing executive for a mutual fund company, while her father, Scott Kingsley Swift, was a financial advisor. Both parents encouraged Taylor's passion for music and played a significant role in her early development as an artist.

Swift began showing interest in music when she was only a child, learning to play the piano at the age of five. By the time she was ten, she had picked up the guitar, and her love for songwriting began to take shape. Throughout her early years, Taylor was influenced by an array of artists from different genres, ranging from country legends like Dolly Parton, Shania Twain, and the Dixie Chicks to pop icons such as Britney Spears and Christina Aguilera.

Her early exposure to country music played a particularly significant role in shaping her initial sound and storytelling approach. Swift has often credited her admiration for singer-songwriter Faith Hill as a key factor in her decision to pursue a career in country music. Additionally, the narrative-driven nature of country music inspired Swift to adopt a confessional songwriting style that would later become her signature.

As she honed her craft, Swift started performing at local venues, talent shows, and county fairs, gradually gaining experience and recognition. By the time she was a teenager, her determination to succeed in the music industry led her and her family to relocate to Nashville, Tennessee, the epicenter of country music. This pivotal move marked the beginning of her journey towards becoming a global music sensation.

In summary, Taylor Swift's introduction to music and early influences were shaped by her supportive family, her exposure to various musical genres, and her passion for storytelling through songwriting. These formative experiences laid the foundation for her unique sound and approach to music that would eventually propel her to superstardom.

C. Pursuit of a career in the music industry

Taylor Swift's pursuit of a career in the music industry began at a young age, fueled by her passion for performing and her love of country music. Her parents recognized her talent and provided her with the necessary support and resources to develop her skills, which would later prove to be invaluable in her journey to stardom.

At the age of ten, Swift began performing at local events, karaoke contests, and county fairs. This exposure to the world of live performance allowed her to hone her stage presence and gain valuable experience in front of audiences. Additionally, she started to learn the guitar, a skill that would become integral to her identity as a singer-songwriter.

In her early teens, Swift began to write her own songs, drawing inspiration from her personal experiences and emotions. Her talent for storytelling and her unique perspective on life were evident in her lyrics, setting her apart from other aspiring artists.

Recognizing the importance of being in the epicenter of the country music scene, Swift and her family made the bold decision to move to Nashville, Tennessee, when she was just 14 years old. This relocation provided her with unparalleled access to the music industry and allowed her to network with important figures within the country music community.

Once in Nashville, Swift's persistence and determination began to pay off. She frequently performed at local venues and songwriter showcases, catching the attention of industry executives and music producers. At the age of 15, she signed a publishing deal with Sony/ATV, making her the youngest songwriter ever signed by the company.

Swift's big break came when she was discovered by Scott Borchetta, who was in the process of starting his own label, Big Machine Records. Impressed by her talent and potential, Borchetta signed Swift to his label, giving her the opportunity to record and release her first album.

In 2006, at the age of 16, Taylor Swift released her self-titled debut album, marking the official start of her career in the music industry. The album was a critical and commercial success, propelling Swift into the spotlight and setting the stage for her future as a global pop icon.

In summary, Taylor Swift's pursuit of a career in the music industry was characterized by her unwavering determination, passion for music, and strong family support. Her early exposure to performing, combined with her move to Nashville and her undeniable talent, allowed her to achieve success in the competitive world of music and become the influential artist she is today.

D. Challenges faced in her initial years

In the early years of her career, Taylor Swift encountered a series of challenges that tested her determination and resilience. These obstacles, although daunting, played a pivotal role in shaping her into the remarkable artist she is today.

Navigating the music industry as a young and aspiring artist was not without its difficulties. Taylor faced skepticism from industry insiders who doubted her ability to make a significant impact. Many were hesitant to invest in a teenage singer-songwriter, questioning her maturity and marketability.

Additionally, breaking into the music scene required Taylor to confront rejection and setbacks. She tirelessly performed at local venues, often to small and indifferent crowds. These experiences taught her the value of persistence and honed her ability to connect with audiences, no matter the size.

Balancing her music career with the demands of school and personal life posed another challenge. Taylor Swift was determined to finish her education while pursuing her dreams, showcasing her commitment to her craft and her dedication to her studies.

As a young artist, Taylor also had to overcome the pressures of self-doubt and societal expectations. The fear of failure and the weight of public scrutiny were constant companions on her journey. However, these challenges only fueled her drive to prove herself and shatter stereotypes.

Despite these obstacles, Taylor Swift's unwavering passion, unparalleled talent, and relentless work ethic propelled her forward. She channeled her experiences into her music, using them as a source of inspiration for her heartfelt and relatable lyrics. Through it all, Taylor's resilience and ability to turn adversity into triumphs laid the foundation for her incredible rise to stardom.

The challenges faced by Taylor Swift in her initial years were not merely stumbling blocks; they were stepping stones towards her ultimate success. Her ability to transform setbacks into stepping stones demonstrates the strength of her character and the depth of her artistic integrity. It is this perseverance that makes her story a testament to the power of resilience and the pursuit of one's passions against all odds.

III. BREAKING THROUGH: THE START OF TAYLOR SWIFT'S CAREER

A. *The release of her debut album "Taylor Swift"*

In 2006, Taylor Swift released her self-titled debut album, which marked the beginning of her illustrious career in the music industry. At just 16 years old, Swift showcased her exceptional talent as a singer-songwriter and proved herself to be a formidable force in the world of country music.

"Taylor Swift" was released on October 24, 2006, under the Big Machine Records label, founded by Scott Borchetta. The album was primarily a country record, featuring a blend of contemporary country-pop sounds and traditional country elements. Swift co-wrote all of the songs on the album, working with experienced songwriters such as Liz Rose, Robert Ellis Orrall, and Brian Maher. This collaboration helped her refine her songwriting skills while maintaining her unique voice and perspective.

The album's lead single, "Tim McGraw," was released in June 2006 and quickly gained traction on country radio. The song showcased Swift's storytelling abilities and her penchant for writing deeply personal and relatable lyrics. As a tribute to one of her musical influences, the song demonstrated Swift's ability to connect with her audience through shared experiences and emotions.

Following the success of "Tim McGraw," subsequent singles such as "Teardrops on My Guitar," "Our Song," and "Picture to Burn" further solidified Swift's position as a rising star in country music. These songs highlighted her skill in crafting catchy melodies and memorable choruses, setting the stage for her future crossover success in pop music.

"Taylor Swift" received critical acclaim, with many praising her songwriting abilities and the album's blend of contemporary and traditional country sounds. The album peaked at number five on the Billboard 200 chart and remained on the chart for a remarkable 277 weeks. It was eventually certified 7x Platinum by the RIAA, signifying over seven million units sold in the United States alone.

The success of her debut album earned Swift numerous accolades, including a nomination for Best New Artist at the 50th Annual Grammy Awards. This recognition helped to further establish her as a promising talent in the music industry.

In conclusion, the release of Taylor Swift's debut album marked the beginning of her extraordinary career as a singer-songwriter and country music sensation. The album showcased her impressive talents and set the foundation for her future success as a global pop icon.

B. The success of singles like "Tim McGraw" and "Teardrops on My Guitar"

The release of Taylor Swift's self-titled debut album in 2006 marked the beginning of her ascent to stardom. Among the standout tracks on the album were the singles "Tim McGraw" and "Teardrops on My Guitar," both of which played a crucial role in establishing her presence in the music industry and propelling her to success.

"Tim McGraw" was Swift's debut single, and it showcased her ability to craft poignant, narrative-driven songs that resonated with listeners. The song, which was a heartfelt reflection on a past relationship, demonstrated Swift's maturity and songwriting prowess despite her young age. "Tim McGraw" quickly gained traction on country radio, reaching No. 6 on the Billboard Hot Country Songs chart and No. 40 on the Billboard Hot 100 chart. The single's success caught the attention of both fans and industry professionals, earning her widespread recognition and acclaim.

"Teardrops on My Guitar," the second single from her debut album, further solidified Swift's reputation as a gifted songwriter and performer. The song, which dealt with unrequited love and heartache, struck a chord with many listeners who could relate to its emotional themes. "Teardrops on My Guitar" became an even bigger hit than "Tim McGraw," reaching No. 2 on the Billboard Hot Country Songs chart and No. 13 on the Billboard Hot 100 chart. The song's accompanying music video, which featured Swift's emotive performance, garnered significant airplay on music video channels and further contributed to the single's success.

The success of these two singles played a pivotal role in launching Taylor Swift's career, providing her with a solid foundation upon which to build her future musical endeavors. By connecting with audiences through her heartfelt lyrics and captivating storytelling, Swift quickly established herself as a country music sensation and laid the groundwork for her eventual transition to pop superstardom.

C. Establishing herself as a country music sensation

With the release of her self-titled debut album, Taylor Swift rapidly established herself as a country music sensation. Her unique blend of contemporary and traditional country sounds, combined with her heartfelt lyrics and storytelling abilities, resonated with audiences and earned her a dedicated fan base.

Swift's relatable narratives and down-to-earth persona endeared her to country music fans, who found solace and inspiration in her songs. Her ability to capture the emotions and experiences of everyday life set her apart from other artists, helping her connect with listeners on a deeper level.

As her singles climbed the charts and gained airplay on country radio, Swift's reputation as a talented singer-songwriter and performer continued to grow. Her live performances showcased her charisma, stage presence, and the genuine connection she shared with her audience. These qualities endeared her to fans and critics alike, further cementing her status as a country music sensation.

In addition to her impressive songwriting and vocal abilities, Swift also demonstrated a strong work ethic and a commitment to her craft. She spent countless hours writing, recording, and promoting her music, which contributed to her meteoric rise in the country music scene.

Her success as a country artist did not go unnoticed by the music industry. Swift received numerous awards and accolades for her debut album, including the Academy of Country Music Award for Top New Female Vocalist and the Country Music Association Horizon Award. These honors recognized her contributions to the genre and her potential for long-lasting success.

As Swift continued to release new music, she continued to evolve as an artist. Her sophomore album, "Fearless," which was released in 2008, further solidified her position as a country music powerhouse. The album's blend of country and pop elements served as a precursor to her eventual crossover into the pop music scene.

In summary, Taylor Swift's early years in the music industry were marked by her swift rise to fame as a country music sensation. Her unique sound, captivating storytelling, and undeniable talent earned her the admiration of fans and critics alike, setting the stage for her future success as a global pop icon.

IV. CROSSOVER SUCCESS AND RISE TO SUPERSTARDOM

A. The release of "Fearless" and its massive success

In 2008, Taylor Swift released her highly anticipated sophomore album, "Fearless," which would go on to become a monumental success and a turning point in her career. Building on the momentum of her debut album, Swift continued to showcase her storytelling prowess, creating a collection of relatable and emotive songs that resonated with a wide audience.

"Fearless" debuted at No. 1 on the Billboard 200 chart, solidifying Swift's status as a major force in the music industry. The album's lead single, "Love Story," became an instant hit with its modern take on the classic Romeo and Juliet tale, blending country and pop elements to create a crossover sensation. The song reached No. 4 on the Billboard Hot 100 chart and No. 1 on the Billboard Hot Country Songs chart, showcasing her growing appeal to both country and pop fans.

The album also spawned other successful singles, such as "White Horse," "You Belong with Me," and "Fifteen," each of which showcased Swift's ability to connect with listeners through her candid storytelling and relatable themes. "You Belong with Me," in particular, became one of her most successful singles, reaching No. 2 on the Billboard Hot 100 chart and further expanding her fanbase.

"Fearless" received widespread critical acclaim and went on to win several prestigious awards, including Album of the Year and Best Country Album at the 52nd Annual Grammy Awards in 2010. At just 20 years old, Swift became the youngest artist at the time to win Album of the Year, a testament to her immense talent and impact on the music industry.

The massive success of "Fearless" not only confirmed Taylor Swift's status as a country music star but also paved the way for her eventual transition into pop music. With its record-breaking sales and widespread acclaim, the album marked a significant milestone in Swift's career and set the stage for her continued rise to superstardom.

B. Transition from country
to pop music

Taylor Swift's transition from country to pop music was a gradual and deliberate process, showcasing her versatility as an artist and her ability to adapt to different genres. This evolution allowed her to expand her audience and reach new heights of success while staying true to her roots as a singer-songwriter.

The first hints of Swift's transition to pop music were evident in her second studio album, "Fearless," released in 2008. While still predominantly a country album, "Fearless" incorporated elements of pop, such as catchy hooks and polished production. The album's lead single, "Love Story," demonstrated her ability to create radio-friendly, mainstream hits that appealed to a wider audience.

Swift's third studio album, "Speak Now," released in 2010, continued to blur the lines between country and pop music. Although the album maintained some of her country roots, it featured a more pop-oriented sound with tracks like "Mine" and "Enchanted." As Swift's popularity grew, so did her interest in exploring new musical territories.

The transition to pop music became more pronounced with the release of her fourth studio album, "Red," in 2012. While the album included country-tinged tracks like "Begin Again," it also featured pop anthems such as "We Are Never Ever Getting Back Together" and "I Knew You Were Trouble." The album's diverse sonic landscape showcased Swift's musical growth and her willingness to experiment with different styles.

Swift's full-fledged embrace of pop music came with her fifth studio album, "1989," released in 2014. Described as her first official pop album, "1989" was a departure from her country roots, featuring a synth-pop sound with tracks like "Shake It Off," "Blank

Space," and "Bad Blood." The album received critical acclaim and commercial success, solidifying her status as a pop superstar.

The transition from country to pop music allowed Swift to reinvent herself as an artist and expand her reach to a broader audience. Her ability to evolve and adapt to different genres demonstrated her musical versatility and creativity. Moreover, her continued success in the pop realm proved that she could excel in both country and pop music, further establishing her as one of the most influential and important pop icons of her generation.

In conclusion, Taylor Swift's transition from country to pop music was a pivotal moment in her career, marking a shift in her musical identity and broadening her appeal to a global audience. This evolution showcased her artistic growth, versatility, and her ability to remain relevant in an ever-changing musical landscape.

C. Unprecedented achievements and accolades

Throughout her illustrious career, Taylor Swift has amassed an impressive array of achievements and accolades, setting numerous records and earning widespread recognition for her contributions to the music industry.

Chart-topping success: Swift has consistently topped the charts with her albums and singles, earning numerous No. 1 spots on the Billboard Hot 100, Billboard 200, and other charts. As of 2021, she has had seven albums debut at No. 1 on the Billboard 200 chart, making her one of the few artists to achieve this feat.

Grammy Awards: Swift has won multiple Grammy Awards, including three Album of the Year wins for "Fearless," "1989," and "folklore." With these wins, she became the first woman to win the prestigious Album of the Year award three times, highlighting her significant impact on the music industry.

American Music Awards (AMAs): Swift has won numerous American Music Awards throughout her career, making her one of the most awarded artists in the history of the event. In 2019, she was honored with the Artist of the Decade award, acknowledging her remarkable achievements during the 2010s.

Songwriting accomplishments: As a talented songwriter, Swift has been recognized for her contributions to the craft. She was honored with the Songwriters Hall of Fame's Hal David Starlight Award in 2010 and was named Songwriter of the Year by the Nashville Songwriters Association International in 2007, 2010, and 2013.

Record-breaking album sales: Swift has consistently broken records with her album sales, making her one of the best-selling artists of all time. As of 2021, she has sold over 200 million records worldwide, demonstrating her immense popularity and the enduring appeal of her music.

Global impact: Taylor Swift's influence extends far beyond the United States. Her music has been embraced by fans across the globe, with her albums and singles achieving multi-platinum status in numerous countries.

Philanthropic recognition: In addition to her musical achievements, Swift has been recognized for her philanthropic efforts and activism. In 2012, she was awarded the Ripple of Hope Award by the Robert F. Kennedy Center for her commitment to social change and her work with various charitable organizations.

These unprecedented achievements and accolades are a testament to Taylor Swift's exceptional talent, work ethic, and dedication to her craft. Her remarkable success has firmly established her as one of the most influential and iconic artists of her generation, leaving a lasting impact on the music industry and pop culture as a whole.

V. REDEFINING POP MUSIC

A. The release of "1989" and its impact on the pop music scene

T he release of Taylor Swift's album "1989" marked a seismic shift in the pop music landscape, leaving an indelible mark that continues to resonate to this day. This pivotal moment in her career showcased Taylor's evolution as an artist and solidified her position as a dominant force in the pop music scene.

"1989" was not merely an album; it was a sonic and visual experience that captivated listeners and fans around the world. Departing from her country roots, Taylor Swift embraced a full-fledged pop sound that embraced catchy melodies, infectious hooks, and a contemporary production style. The result was a collection of songs that transcended genres and appealed to a diverse audience, demonstrating her versatility and musical prowess.

The impact of "1989" on the pop music scene was profound and transformative. The album not only marked Taylor's successful transition from country to pop, but it also redefined the very essence of pop music itself. The album's sleek production, irresistible hooks, and relatable lyrics set new standards for what pop music could achieve, inspiring a new generation of artists to experiment with their sound.

Critics and fans alike hailed "1989" as a masterpiece, praising its innovation, authenticity, and emotional depth. The album spawned a series of chart-topping singles, including "Shake It Off," "Blank Space," and "Bad Blood," each accompanied by visually stunning music videos that further solidified Taylor's influence on pop culture.

Beyond its musical impact, "1989" had a profound influence on fashion, aesthetics, and visual storytelling. Taylor Swift's impeccable sense of style and her ability to seamlessly integrate visuals into her music elevated the album into a multimedia experience. From her iconic "1989 World Tour" to her innovative use of social media, Taylor redefined how artists engage with their audience in the digital age.

"1989" not only reinvigorated Taylor Swift's career, but it also ignited a resurgence of interest in the pop genre. Its success served as a blueprint for artists seeking to reinvent themselves and push creative boundaries. The album's legacy endures, serving as a testament to Taylor Swift's ability to continually evolve as an artist while maintaining her authentic voice.

In conclusion, the release of "1989" was a watershed moment in Taylor Swift's career and in the realm of pop music. Its impact on the pop music scene was monumental, reshaping the genre and inspiring a new generation of artists to push artistic boundaries. The album's legacy continues to shine as a beacon of creativity, innovation, and enduring relevance in the ever-changing landscape of popular music.

B. Creation of memorable music videos and live performances

Taylor Swift's music videos are more than just visual accompaniments to her songs; they are cinematic experiences that extend the narrative of her music and provide deeper insight into her creative vision. Each video is meticulously crafted, often laden with symbolism and hidden messages that invite viewers to delve deeper into the world she has created. From the fairy-tale romance of "Love Story" to the vibrant, 80s-inspired aesthetics of "Shake It Off," Swift's music videos have consistently pushed the boundaries of what can be achieved in this medium.

Her music videos often serve as cultural events in their own right. The release of a new Taylor Swift video is always a highly anticipated event, with fans eagerly dissecting every frame for clues and references. This level of engagement is a testament to the thought and care Swift puts into her videos, ensuring they are not just promotional tools, but integral parts of her artistic output.

Swift's live performances, too, are memorable events that showcase her talent and charisma. Whether she's performing in intimate settings or headlining sold-out stadiums, Swift's concerts are experiences that resonate with her audience. Her performances are a blend of musical prowess, theatrical storytelling, and personal connection, creating an atmosphere that captivates and enthralls.

From her energetic performances of pop anthems that get the whole crowd dancing, to the quiet, emotional renditions of her more introspective songs, Swift's concerts are a journey through her musical landscape. They are a testament to her ability to connect with her audience, turning thousands of strangers into a unified crowd singing along to every word.

Moreover, Swift's live performances often feature surprise elements, from unexpected song choices to guest appearances, keeping fans on their toes and adding an element of excitement and unpredictability to her shows. These moments, often shared and celebrated on social media, contribute to the sense of community and shared experience among her fans.

In creating memorable music videos and live performances, Taylor Swift has not only entertained her fans but also enriched their understanding of her music. These visual and live elements allow her to express her creativity in new ways, further solidifying her status as a versatile and innovative artist.

C. Embracing her role as a pop music icon

Following the release of "1989" and her successful transition to pop music, Taylor Swift fully embraced her role as a pop music icon. Her influence and impact extended far beyond her own music, as she became a powerful force in the music industry and a symbol of resilience and reinvention.

As a pop music icon, Swift leveraged her fame and influence to support and mentor emerging artists, helping to shape the careers of many up-and-coming musicians. She also used her platform to champion important causes, such as gender equality, mental health awareness, and artists' rights. These actions solidified her position as a role model and an advocate for change in the music industry.

Swift's live performances and music videos played a crucial role in her evolution as a pop music icon. Her visually stunning and meticulously planned shows incorporated elaborate set designs, choreography, and special effects, creating memorable experiences for her fans. These performances showcased her dedication to her craft and her ability to captivate audiences around the world.

In addition to her music, Swift's fashion choices and personal style also contributed to her status as a pop icon. She became known for her bold and distinctive outfits, often drawing inspiration from the themes and aesthetics of her albums. Her fashion choices resonated with fans and influenced popular culture, further expanding her impact on the world of pop music.

Swift's interactions with her fans played a significant role in her rise to icon status. She maintained a close relationship with her fanbase, often engaging with them on social media and at live events. This connection fostered a sense of community among her fans and demonstrated her genuine appreciation for their support.

As a pop music icon, Swift also inspired countless aspiring musicians, who looked up to her as a role model and a symbol of perseverance. Her journey from a country music sensation to a global pop superstar illustrated the importance of self-belief, hard work, and determination in achieving success.

In conclusion, Taylor Swift's embrace of her role as a pop music icon has had a profound impact on the music industry and popular culture. Her dedication to her craft, her support for emerging artists, and her advocacy for important causes have solidified her status as a true icon and a driving force in the world of pop music.

VI. THE ART OF SONGWRITING

A. Taylor Swift's approach
to songwriting

Taylor Swift's songwriting is a cornerstone of her success and a key element of her artistic identity. Her approach to songwriting is deeply personal, often drawing from her own experiences and emotions. This authenticity resonates with her audience, allowing them to connect with her music on a profound level.

Swift's songwriting process begins with an idea, a concept, or a single line that captures her attention. She has often spoken about how her best songs come to her quickly, almost fully formed. However, she also emphasizes the importance of patience and persistence, acknowledging that some songs require more time and effort to take shape.

Swift is known for her narrative songwriting style. Her songs often tell stories, complete with characters, settings, and plotlines. This storytelling approach makes her music relatable and engaging, inviting listeners to immerse themselves in the world she has created. From the youthful romance of "Love Story" to the introspective reflection of "All Too Well," Swift's songs are narratives that capture specific moments and emotions.

One of Swift's most distinctive songwriting traits is her use of detail. She has a knack for incorporating specific, vivid details into her lyrics, which makes her songs feel intimate and real. These details, whether they're references to a little black dress or a scarf left at a sister's house, add depth and richness to her music.

Swift also uses her songwriting to explore complex emotions and experiences. Her songs tackle themes of love, heartbreak, friendship, fame, and self-discovery, among others. She is unafraid to delve into difficult or painful experiences, using her music as a form of catharsis and a means of processing her feelings.

In her approach to songwriting, Taylor Swift combines personal authenticity, narrative storytelling, and attention to detail to create music that is deeply resonant and emotionally powerful. Her songwriting prowess has not only contributed to her success as an artist but also established her as a significant voice in contemporary music.

B. The stories behind some
of her biggest hits

Taylor Swift's songs are renowned for their narrative depth and emotional resonance, often drawing from her personal experiences. Here are the stories behind some of her biggest hits:

"Love Story": One of Swift's earliest hits, "Love Story," was inspired by a love interest who wasn't popular with her family and friends. Drawing parallels with the timeless tale of Romeo and Juliet, Swift spun a narrative of forbidden love, but with a happier ending, capturing the hearts of listeners worldwide.

"Mean": This song was Swift's response to a critic who harshly criticized her performance at the 2010 Grammy Awards. The critic suggested that the off-key performance would end her career. Swift channeled her feelings into "Mean," a song about overcoming negativity and proving doubters wrong. It became a powerful anthem for anyone who has ever been bullied or belittled.

"Shake It Off": This upbeat track was Swift's way of dealing with the criticism and scrutiny that come with fame. The song encourages listeners to shake off the haters and negativity, embodying Swift's philosophy of not letting external opinions define her.

"All Too Well": Often hailed as one of Swift's best songs, "All Too Well" is a deeply emotional track rumored to be about her relationship with actor Jake Gyllenhaal. The song's vivid lyrics and emotional depth showcase Swift's songwriting prowess and ability to convey complex emotions through music.

"Blank Space": This song was Swift's satirical take on her media portrayal as a serial dater. Instead of denying the accusations, Swift played into the caricature, creating a song that both mocks and embraces the image created by the media.

These stories behind Swift's songs reveal her ability to transform personal experiences and emotions into universal narratives, making her music relatable to a wide range of listeners.

C. Her evolution as a songwriter over the years

Taylor Swift's evolution as a songwriter mirrors her journey as an artist and a person. From her early days as a country singer-songwriter to her current status as a global pop icon, her songwriting has matured and evolved, reflecting her personal growth and expanding worldview.

In her early career, Swift's songs were deeply rooted in her personal experiences as a teenager. Her lyrics were filled with vivid details and narratives about high school romances, friendships, and heartbreaks. Songs like "Teardrops on My Guitar" and "Fifteen" encapsulate this period of her songwriting, offering a poignant and relatable look at adolescence.

As Swift transitioned into the pop realm with albums like "Red" and "1989," her songwriting also underwent a significant transformation. While she continued to draw from her personal experiences, her lyrics became more universal, exploring broader themes of love, loss, and self-discovery. This period saw the creation of anthems like "Shake It Off" and "Blank Space," which showcased her ability to craft catchy, pop-oriented tunes without losing her narrative depth.

Swift's more recent work, particularly her "folklore" and "evermore" albums, represents another shift in her songwriting. These albums see Swift moving away from the pop sound of her previous records and embracing a more indie, alternative style. Her lyrics have become more introspective and complex, often veering into the realm of the imaginary and the speculative. Songs like "cardigan" and "the last great american dynasty" demonstrate her ability to weave intricate narratives that blur the lines between reality and fiction.

Throughout her evolution as a songwriter, Swift has maintained her authenticity and narrative depth, continually finding new ways to express her experiences and emotions through music. Her ability to adapt and grow as a songwriter has played a crucial role in her longevity and success in the music industry.

VII. PERSONAL LIFE AND RELATIONSHIPS

A. Romantic relationships and the media's scrutiny

Throughout her career, Taylor Swift's romantic relationships have been a subject of intense media scrutiny. The public's fascination with her personal life, along with the media's relentless coverage of her relationships, has been a significant aspect of her life as a pop icon.

Swift has been linked to various high-profile celebrities, including actors, musicians, and other public figures. Each time a new relationship emerged, the media and the public alike took a keen interest in dissecting every aspect of it. This constant attention often led to invasive coverage, unfounded rumors, and speculation about her love life.

The media's scrutiny of Swift's relationships was further fueled by her penchant for writing songs inspired by her personal experiences. Many of her hits, such as "We Are Never Ever Getting Back Together," "I Knew You Were Trouble," and "Style," have been interpreted as being about her past relationships. This connection between her music and her personal life added another layer of intrigue for both fans and the media, leading to attempts to decipher the inspiration behind her songs.

While Swift has been open about using her experiences as material for her music, the excessive focus on her romantic relationships has sometimes overshadowed her artistic achievements. This media obsession has often perpetuated unfair narratives and stereotypes about her as a serial dater or someone who is unable to maintain a stable relationship.

Despite the intense scrutiny and pressure that comes with being in the public eye, Swift has managed to maintain her dignity and composure. She has addressed the media's portrayal of her love life in her music, notably in songs like "Shake It Off" and "Blank Space," where she cleverly uses satire to challenge the misconceptions about her.

In conclusion, Taylor Swift's romantic relationships and the media's scrutiny have been an undeniable aspect of her life as a pop icon. However, Swift has navigated these challenges with grace and resilience, using her music to address misconceptions and share her side of the story. This ability to rise above the noise and stay focused on her artistry is a testament to her strength as an artist and a person.

B. Friendship with other celebrities and the creation of her "squad"

Taylor Swift's friendships with other celebrities have been a significant aspect of her public persona. Her circle of friends, often referred to as her "squad," has included a variety of high-profile figures from the worlds of music, fashion, and film.

In the mid-2010s, Swift's squad was a hot topic in the media. The group included stars like Selena Gomez, Ed Sheeran, Gigi Hadid, Camila Cabello, and Cara Delevingne. These friendships were often showcased in public outings and social media posts, creating a sense of camaraderie and mutual support.

Swift's squad was not just about friendship; it also represented a form of female empowerment. By publicly celebrating her friendships with other successful women, Swift challenged the narrative of female competition and rivalry often perpetuated in the media.

However, over the years, the visibility of Swift's squad has diminished. This change reflects Swift's evolving approach to privacy and her desire to maintain genuine relationships away from the public eye. Despite this shift, Swift continues to maintain close friendships with many celebrities. She often expresses her appreciation for her friends and their support, highlighting the importance of these relationships in her life.

Swift's friendships and the creation of her squad have played a significant role in her journey, offering a support system and a sense of community amidst the pressures of fame. These relationships have also influenced her music, providing inspiration for many of her songs.

C. Balancing fame, privacy, and personal growth

As one of the most recognizable figures in the music industry, Taylor Swift has had to navigate the delicate balance between fame, privacy, and personal growth. This balance is a recurring theme in her life and work, shaping her experiences and influencing her music.

Swift's rise to fame was meteoric, thrusting her into the public eye at a young age. The intense scrutiny that came with fame was a challenge, with every aspect of her life, from her relationships to her personal beliefs, becoming fodder for public discussion. Swift has often spoken about the pressures of living in the public eye and the impact it has had on her life.

Despite the challenges, Swift has managed to maintain a level of privacy that is rare for someone of her fame. She has been strategic about what she shares with the public, choosing to express herself primarily through her music. This approach has allowed her to retain a sense of control over her narrative, even as she navigates the often-invasive world of celebrity.

Swift's journey has also been marked by significant personal growth. As she has matured, so too has her understanding of fame and its implications. She has learned to set boundaries and prioritize her well-being, using her experiences to fuel her creativity and inform her music.

Balancing fame, privacy, and personal growth is a complex task, but Swift has managed it with grace and resilience. Her journey offers valuable insights into the realities of fame and the importance of maintaining one's authenticity amidst the pressures of the spotlight.

VIII. OVERCOMING ADVERSITY

A. Struggles with media portrayal and public opinion

As one of the world's most famous pop stars, Taylor Swift has faced her share of struggles with media portrayal and public opinion. The intense scrutiny of her personal life, relationships, and actions has often led to misrepresentations and unfair criticisms, creating challenges for her both personally and professionally.

The media's portrayal of Swift's romantic relationships, as previously discussed, has been a significant source of struggle. The constant focus on her love life and the perpetuation of unflattering narratives have sometimes threatened to overshadow her artistic accomplishments and her contributions to the music industry.

Additionally, Swift has faced criticism and backlash for her friendships and social circle, which includes other celebrities and influential figures. Dubbed her "squad," the group has been criticized for promoting exclusivity and for being a calculated attempt to boost her public image. While Swift has maintained that her friendships are genuine, the media's portrayal of her social circle has been another source of public scrutiny.

Swift's feud with Kanye West and Kim Kardashian, which began with West interrupting her acceptance speech at the 2009 MTV Video Music Awards, was another high-profile incident that affected her public image. The feud resurfaced in 2016 when West released a song containing controversial lyrics about Swift, leading to a highly publicized disagreement about whether she had approved the lyrics. The incident resulted in a significant backlash against Swift, with many questioning her honesty and integrity.

In response to these struggles with media portrayal and public opinion, Swift has often turned to her music as a way to express her feelings and share her perspective. Her album "Reputation," released in 2017, was a powerful exploration of her experiences with the media, public opinion, and the darker side of fame. Songs like "Look What You Made Me Do" and "Delicate" addressed her struggles head-on, demonstrating her resilience and her determination to rise above the negativity.

Over the years, Taylor Swift has learned to navigate the challenges of fame, media portrayal, and public opinion. By staying true to herself and using her music as an outlet for self-expression, she has managed to overcome these obstacles and continue to thrive as an artist and a pop icon. Her journey serves as an inspiration for others in the public eye and demonstrates the importance of resilience and self-belief in the face of adversity.

B. The feud with Kanye West
and Kim Kardashian

The feud between Taylor Swift, Kanye West, and Kim Kardashian is one of the most publicized celebrity disputes in recent years. The conflict, which spans over a decade, has had several twists and turns, with each party presenting their side of the story.

The feud began at the 2009 MTV Video Music Awards when West interrupted Swift's acceptance speech for Best Female Video to proclaim that Beyoncé should have won the award. This incident sparked a public outcry and marked the beginning of a long-standing conflict between Swift and West.

The feud escalated in 2016 with the release of West's song "Famous," which included a controversial lyric about Swift. West claimed that Swift had approved the lyric, a claim that Swift vehemently denied. The situation became more complicated when Kim Kardashian, West's wife, released snippets of a phone call between West and Swift that seemed to suggest Swift had indeed approved the lyric.

However, the feud reignited in 2020 when the full footage of the phone call was leaked online, revealing that West had not fully disclosed the nature of the lyric to Swift during their conversation. This revelation led to a renewed public debate about the feud and its implications.

The feud between Swift, West, and Kardashian is more than just a celebrity dispute. It raises questions about consent, manipulation, and the power dynamics at play in the music industry. Despite the challenges and controversies, Swift has managed to navigate the situation with resilience, using her music and public platform to express her perspective and stand up for herself.

C. The release of "Reputation" and
its portrayal of her experiences

"Reputation," Taylor Swift's sixth studio album, was released on November 10, 2017. The album marked a significant departure from her previous work, both musically and thematically. With "Reputation," Swift delved into darker, edgier sounds and explored her experiences with media portrayal, public opinion, and the challenges that come with being one of the world's most famous pop stars.

The album's lead single, "Look What You Made Me Do," made it clear that Swift was taking a new direction with her music. The song, accompanied by a visually striking music video, was a biting commentary on her public image and the media's portrayal of her. With lyrics like "I don't trust nobody, and nobody trusts me," Swift highlighted the impact of the media's constant scrutiny and the way it shaped her relationships and reputation.

Other songs on the album, such as "Delicate," addressed the vulnerability that comes with fame and the difficulty of maintaining authentic connections in the face of public scrutiny. In "End Game," featuring Ed Sheeran and Future, Swift discussed her desire to rise above the drama and negativity and focus on what truly matters in her life.

"Reputation" also included tracks that touched upon her romantic relationships, such as "Call It What You Want" and "New Year's Day." These songs provided an intimate glimpse into her personal life, showcasing her growth and maturity as both an artist and an individual.

The album's darker, more aggressive sound was a reflection of Swift's experiences and the way she felt about her public image at the time. The production, featuring heavier beats and electronic elements, added to the overall atmosphere of the album and further distinguished it from her previous work.

"Reputation" received critical acclaim and commercial success, debuting at number one on the Billboard 200 chart and eventually becoming the best-selling album of 2017 in the United States. Its success was a testament to Swift's ability to reinvent herself and her music, as well as her skill in connecting with her audience through honest and authentic storytelling.

In conclusion, the release of "Reputation" and its portrayal of Taylor Swift's experiences provided a powerful insight into her struggles with media portrayal, public opinion, and the challenges of fame. The album showcased her resilience and determination to rise above adversity, while also demonstrating her ability to evolve as an artist and captivate her fans with her unique perspective and storytelling.

IX. PHILANTHROPY AND ACTIVISM

A. Support for charitable organizations and causes

Taylor Swift's philanthropy is as impressive as her music career. She has consistently used her platform to support various charitable organizations and causes, making significant contributions both financially and through advocacy.

Swift has donated millions of dollars to various causes over the years. These include disaster relief efforts, education initiatives, and healthcare institutions. For instance, she has made substantial donations to Vanderbilt University Medical Centre and several food banks, demonstrating her commitment to supporting community services and healthcare.

Swift's philanthropy extends beyond financial contributions. She is also an advocate for several social issues, including LGBTQ rights and women's empowerment. By speaking out about these issues and lending her support, Swift uses her influence to raise awareness and drive change.

Swift's philanthropic efforts are a testament to her belief in giving back and using her fame for good. Her ongoing support for charitable organizations and causes reflects her commitment to making a positive impact on the world.

B. Advocacy for women's rights and gender equality

In addition to her success as a pop icon, Taylor Swift has also used her platform to advocate for women's rights and gender equality. By speaking out on these issues and lending her support to various causes, Swift has demonstrated her commitment to creating a more equitable society and empowering women around the world.

One notable instance of Swift's advocacy for women's rights occurred during her 2017 sexual assault trial. After being sued by a former radio DJ whom she accused of groping her during a meet-and-greet, Swift countersued for a symbolic $1, asserting her right to stand up against sexual assault. The trial garnered widespread attention, and Swift's stance was seen as a powerful statement against victim-blaming and in support of survivors.

Swift has also been vocal about the gender pay gap and the importance of equal pay for equal work. In a 2015 interview with TIME magazine, she stated, "We need to continue to change the conversation and make sure that women are being paid fairly for their work." Swift has consistently used her influence to shed light on this issue and promote fair compensation for all workers, regardless of their gender.

In her music, Swift has addressed themes related to women's empowerment and self-worth. Songs like "The Man," from her 2019 album "Lover," tackle gender double standards and the different ways society treats men and women in positions of power. By incorporating these themes into her music, Swift raises awareness about gender inequality and encourages her fans to join the conversation.

Taylor Swift has also supported various organizations and

initiatives that focus on women's rights and gender equality. She has donated to charities such as the Time's Up Legal Defense Fund, which provides legal assistance to victims of sexual harassment and assault in the workplace, and the Joyful Heart Foundation, which supports survivors of sexual assault, domestic violence, and child abuse.

Swift's advocacy for women's rights and gender equality extends to her support of fellow female artists in the music industry. She has consistently championed and collaborated with other women, helping to create a more inclusive and supportive environment within the industry.

In summary, Taylor Swift's advocacy for women's rights and gender equality is a significant aspect of her work as a pop icon. By using her platform to raise awareness and promote change, she is helping to create a more equitable and just society for everyone. Her commitment to these issues demonstrates her dedication to not only her own success but also the empowerment and well-being of women everywhere.

C. Political involvement and
public stance on various issues

Taylor Swift's political involvement has evolved significantly over the years. Initially, she was known for maintaining a neutral stance on political matters, a decision that drew criticism from some quarters who felt she should use her platform to speak out. However, in recent years, Swift has become increasingly vocal about her political views and has taken a stand on several key issues.

One of the most notable instances of Swift's political activism was her endorsement of two Democratic candidates in the 2018 midterm elections in Tennessee. This marked a significant shift for Swift, who had previously refrained from making political endorsements. Her decision to speak out was praised by many, although it also sparked controversy and debate.

Swift has also been an advocate for LGBTQ rights. She has publicly expressed her support for the community and has spoken out against discriminatory legislation. In 2019, she released the song "You Need to Calm Down," which celebrates the LGBTQ community and criticizes homophobia. The music video for the song features a number of prominent LGBTQ celebrities and ends with a call to sign a petition in support of the Equality Act.

In addition to her political endorsements and advocacy, Swift has also used her music to comment on political and social issues. Her album "folklore" has been interpreted as containing political commentary, while her documentary "Miss Americana" also touches on her political awakening.

Swift's political involvement demonstrates her commitment to using her platform to effect change. While her decision to speak out politically has been met with mixed reactions, it has undoubtedly contributed to important conversations and has shown her fans and the public that she is not afraid to stand up for what she believes in.

D. Influence on fans and using her platform for good

As a global pop icon, Taylor Swift has amassed a dedicated fanbase known as "Swifties." Her influence on her fans extends beyond her music, as she uses her platform to promote positive messages, advocate for important causes, and inspire her fans to make a difference in their own lives and the world around them.

One of the ways Swift connects with her fans is through social media, where she shares updates about her life, her thoughts on various issues, and messages of support and encouragement. By engaging with her fans in a genuine and authentic manner, she fosters a sense of community and belonging among her followers.

Swift also uses her platform to raise awareness about mental health and self-care. She has been open about her own struggles with anxiety and the importance of seeking help when needed. By discussing these topics, she helps to break the stigma surrounding mental health and encourages her fans to prioritize their well-being.

Additionally, Swift has been a vocal advocate for education and the importance of reading and writing. She has donated books to schools and libraries and has supported literacy programs, inspiring her fans to value education and develop their own love for reading and writing.

Moreover, Swift has used her influence to promote social and political causes that she believes in. She has encouraged her fans to vote and engage in the democratic process, stressing the importance of making their voices heard. By doing so, she has helped inspire a new generation of politically engaged and socially conscious young people.

In times of crisis, Swift has also shown her commitment to helping those in need. She has donated significant amounts of money to disaster relief efforts, such as the Nashville flood in 2010, Hurricane Harvey in 2017, and the Australian bushfires in 2020. These actions demonstrate her compassion and willingness to use her resources to help others.

Through her philanthropic work, advocacy, and personal engagement with her fans, Taylor Swift has shown a genuine commitment to using her platform for good. By leveraging her fame and influence, she has inspired countless fans to become more socially conscious, compassionate, and engaged in their communities. In doing so, Swift has not only solidified her status as a pop icon but also established herself as a powerful force for positive change in the world.

X. THE "TAYLOR'S VERSION" ERA

A. The decision to re-record her old albums

Taylor Swift's decision to re-record her old albums marked a significant moment in her career. This decision was driven by a dispute over the ownership of her master recordings, which are the original recordings of her songs.

In 2019, Swift's former record label, Big Machine Records, sold her back catalogue to a private equity firm. This sale meant that Swift no longer had control over her master recordings, which included her first six albums. Swift was deeply upset by this sale, as she had not been given the opportunity to buy her own masters.

In response to this situation, Swift made the decision to re-record her old albums. By doing so, she would regain control over her music, as she would own the rights to these new recordings. This move was not only a strategic business decision but also a powerful statement about artists' rights and the importance of owning one's work.

Swift's re-recordings, known as "Taylor's Version" albums, have been met with widespread acclaim. They have allowed her to revisit her old music and present it in a way that reflects her growth as an artist. Moreover, they have given her the opportunity to take control of her musical legacy and ensure that her work is handled in a way that aligns with her wishes.

B. The impact and reception of "Taylor's Version" albums

The release of Taylor Swift's "Taylor's Version" albums has had a significant impact on both her career and the music industry at large. The re-recorded albums have been met with widespread acclaim from critics and fans alike, further solidifying Swift's status as one of the most influential artists of her generation.

The first of these albums, "Fearless (Taylor's Version)," was praised for its faithful recreation of the original while also offering something new. The album was a commercial success, demonstrating that Swift's decision to re-record her music was not only a powerful symbolic gesture but also a sound business move.

The subsequent "Taylor's Version" albums, including "Red (Taylor's Version)" and "Speak Now (Taylor's Version)," have also been well-received. They have allowed Swift to revisit her earlier work and reinterpret it through the lens of her current artistic perspective. These albums have also given fans the opportunity to rediscover Swift's music and appreciate the depth and evolution of her songwriting.

Beyond their commercial and critical success, the "Taylor's Version" albums have had a broader impact on the music industry. They have sparked conversations about artists' rights and the importance of owning one's work, challenging the traditional power dynamics within the industry. Swift's decision to re-record her albums has set a precedent that could potentially influence other artists in similar situations, making the "Taylor's Version" era a significant moment in music history.

C. The significance of this move in the music industry

Taylor Swift's decision to re-record her old albums has had a profound impact on the music industry. This move has not only been a significant step for Swift's career but has also sparked important conversations about artists' rights and the music industry's power dynamics.

Swift's re-recordings have challenged the traditional structures of the music industry. Typically, record labels own the master recordings of an artist's songs, giving them control over the music's distribution and profits. However, by re-recording her music, Swift has regained control over her work, setting a precedent for other artists who may find themselves in similar situations.

This move has also highlighted the importance of artists owning their master recordings. Swift's dispute with her former record label over the ownership of her masters has brought attention to this often-overlooked aspect of the music industry. It has sparked discussions about the fairness of record contracts and the need for greater transparency and equity in the industry.

Furthermore, Swift's re-recordings have demonstrated the power of artists in the digital age. With the rise of streaming platforms and social media, artists like Swift have more control over their music and their careers than ever before. Swift's decision to re-record her albums is a testament to this power and the changing dynamics of the music industry.

In conclusion, Swift's "Taylor's Version" era is not just a significant moment in her career, but a pivotal moment in music history. It represents a shift in the industry's power dynamics and a step towards greater artist autonomy.

XI. THE POWER OF FANDOM: SWIFTIES

A. The formation and growth of her fanbase

Taylor Swift's fanbase, affectionately known as the "Swifties," has been a significant part of her journey as an artist. The formation and growth of this fanbase have been influenced by various factors, including Swift's music, her public persona, and her interactions with her fans.

Swift's fanbase began to form with the release of her debut album, "Taylor Swift," in 2006. Her relatable lyrics and catchy melodies quickly attracted a following, particularly among young listeners. As Swift's music evolved, so too did her fanbase, growing to encompass a diverse range of ages, backgrounds, and identities.

Swift's relationship with her fans has also played a crucial role in the growth of her fanbase. She is known for her direct and personal interactions with her fans, whether through social media, fan events, or surprise "Swiftmas" gifts. These interactions have fostered a sense of community among Swifties and have deepened their connection with Swift.

The growth of Swift's fanbase has also been influenced by her evolution as an artist. As Swift has explored different genres and themes in her music, she has attracted new listeners while also retaining her core fanbase. This ability to evolve while maintaining her connection with her fans is a testament to Swift's artistry and her understanding of her audience.

In conclusion, the formation and growth of Swift's fanbase have been integral to her success as an artist. The Swifties are more than just fans; they are a community that supports and celebrates Swift, contributing to her enduring impact in the music industry.

B. Her relationship with her fans

Taylor Swift's relationship with her fans, known as "Swifties," is a unique and integral aspect of her career. Swift has cultivated a close bond with her fans, often referring to them as her "friends" rather than just supporters. This relationship has been built on mutual respect and admiration, with Swift often going out of her way to interact with her fans.

Swift is known for her direct and personal interactions with her fans. She frequently communicates with them on social media, shares details about her life and music, and even surprises them with gifts. These actions have fostered a sense of intimacy and connection between Swift and her fans, making them feel seen and appreciated.

This relationship is not just one-sided. Swift's fans have shown their support for her in various ways, from attending her concerts and buying her music to defending her in public disputes. Their loyalty and dedication have been a significant source of strength for Swift throughout her career.

However, Swift's relationship with her fans is not without its complexities. The intense connection between Swift and her fans can sometimes blur the lines between the personal and the public, leading to what some have termed "parasocial relationships." These are one-sided relationships where fans feel a close connection to a celebrity, even though the celebrity may not know them personally.

Despite these complexities, Swift's relationship with her fans remains a defining aspect of her career. It is a testament to her ability to connect with her audience on a deep level, making them feel valued and part of her journey.

C. The role of her fans in her success

Taylor Swift's fans, affectionately known as "Swifties," have played an instrumental role in her success. Their unwavering support and dedication have not only contributed to her commercial success but have also shaped her career in significant ways.

Swift's fans have been a driving force behind her music's popularity. They have shown their support by buying her albums, attending her concerts, and engaging with her on social media. This support has helped Swift achieve numerous chart-topping hits and sell-out tours, contributing to her status as one of the most successful artists of her generation.

Moreover, Swift's fans have stood by her during challenging times, such as her dispute with her former record label and public feuds. Their loyalty during these times has provided Swift with a sense of stability and support, enabling her to navigate these challenges with confidence.

Swift's fans have also played a role in shaping her music. Swift is known for her close relationship with her fans and often incorporates their feedback into her work. This connection has allowed Swift to create music that resonates with her audience, further strengthening her bond with her fans.

In conclusion, Swift's fans have played a crucial role in her success. Their support has not only contributed to her commercial achievements but has also provided her with a supportive community that has shaped her career in profound ways.

XII. TAYLOR SWIFT AND THE MEDIA

A. Her relationship with the media over the years

Taylor Swift's relationship with the media has been a complex and evolving one. From her early days as a country music star to her current status as a global pop icon, Swift's interactions with the media have played a significant role in shaping her public image.

In the early stages of her career, Swift was often portrayed as the girl-next-door, with her relatable lyrics and wholesome image resonating with a wide audience. However, as her fame grew, so did media scrutiny. Her personal life, particularly her romantic relationships, became a frequent topic of media coverage, often overshadowing her musical achievements.

The media's focus on her personal life led to a shift in Swift's relationship with the press. She began to take control of her narrative, using her music and social media to communicate directly with her fans. This approach allowed her to bypass traditional media channels and present her perspective on her terms.

Swift's relationship with the media took another turn following the dispute over her master recordings. The controversy was widely covered in the press, with Swift using the media attention to highlight issues of artists' rights in the music industry.

Over the years, Swift's relationship with the media has been marked by both cooperation and conflict. However, through it all, she has managed to navigate the media landscape with resilience and savvy, using it as a tool to connect with her fans and advocate for her beliefs.

B. The impact of media scrutiny on her life and career

Media scrutiny has had a significant impact on Taylor Swift's life and career. As her fame grew, so did the intensity of the media's focus on her, with her personal life often becoming a topic of public discussion. This scrutiny has affected Swift in various ways, influencing her music, her public image, and her personal life.

The media's focus on Swift's romantic relationships has been a recurring theme throughout her career. This scrutiny has often overshadowed her musical achievements and has led to a significant amount of public speculation and commentary. Swift has addressed this issue in her music, using her songs to express her feelings and tell her side of the story.

Media scrutiny has also played a role in some of the challenges Swift has faced in her career. Public feuds and controversies have been amplified by the media, adding to the pressure and criticism Swift has faced. However, Swift has shown resilience in the face of this scrutiny, using these experiences as fuel for her music and as opportunities to stand up for herself and her beliefs.

Moreover, the media scrutiny has led Swift to be more guarded about her privacy. She has taken steps to protect her personal life from public scrutiny, such as keeping her relationships out of the public eye and being more selective about her media appearances.

In conclusion, media scrutiny has had a profound impact on Swift's life and career. While it has presented challenges, it has also shaped her as an artist and as a person. Through it all, Swift has navigated the media landscape with resilience and grace, using her experiences to create music that resonates with her fans and stands up for what she believes in.

C. Her strategies for managing
her public image

Taylor Swift's strategies for managing her public image have been a key factor in her enduring success and relevance in the music industry. Swift has demonstrated a keen understanding of how to navigate the public sphere, using a combination of authenticity, strategic brand collaborations, and savvy image shifts to maintain her appeal.

One of Swift's most notable strategies is her authentic storytelling. Through her music and public interactions, Swift presents herself as a genuine and relatable figure. This authenticity resonates with her fans, helping to build a strong and loyal fanbase.

Swift also strategically collaborates with various brands, aligning herself with companies and causes that reflect her values and image. These collaborations not only enhance her public image but also allow her to reach a wider audience.

Another key strategy is Swift's ability to shift her image in line with the evolution of her music. Each new album brings with it a new era, complete with a distinct aesthetic and narrative. These image shifts keep her fan base interested and engaged, while also attracting new listeners.

Swift is also known for her business savvy. She has built a strong brand for her music and herself, using well-defined strategies to manage her public image. This includes taking control of her narrative during controversies and using her platform to advocate for artists' rights.

In conclusion, Swift's strategies for managing her public image are a testament to her understanding of the media landscape and her ability to adapt and evolve. These strategies have played a crucial role in her success, helping her to maintain her relevance and appeal in the ever-changing music industry.

XIII. TAYLOR SWIFT'S IMPACT ON SOCIAL MEDIA

A. Her use of social media platforms

Taylor Swift's use of social media platforms has been a key element of her connection with fans and her overall brand strategy. Swift has a significant presence on various platforms, including Instagram, Twitter, Tumblr, and TikTok, each of which she uses in unique ways to engage with her audience.

Swift is known for her immersive approach to Instagram, often sharing behind-the-scenes content and personal moments that give fans a glimpse into her life. She also uses Instagram stories to create a more interactive experience for her fans.

On Twitter, Swift engages with fans through tweets and replies, often using the platform to share news and updates about her music. She's also known for "creeping" on her fans' Twitter accounts, a practice that has endeared her to her audience.

Swift's use of Tumblr is particularly noteworthy. Unlike more public platforms, Tumblr is seen by its users as a community, and Swift has embraced this aspect of the platform. She frequently interacts with fans on Tumblr, reblogging their posts and even responding to their questions and comments.

Swift also has a significant presence on TikTok, where she shares short videos and clips, often related to her music. This platform allows her to reach a younger demographic and engage with fans in a more casual and creative way.

In conclusion, Swift's use of social media platforms is a testament to her understanding of the digital landscape and her ability to connect with her audience in diverse and meaningful ways.

B. The influence of her
social media presence

Taylor Swift's social media presence has had a profound influence on her career, her fans, and the music industry at large. Her strategic use of various platforms has not only amplified her reach but also reshaped how artists engage with their fans and market their work.

Swift's social media presence has been instrumental in promoting her music and brand. She often uses her platforms to announce new music, share behind-the-scenes content, and promote her tours and merchandise. This direct line of communication allows her to market her work effectively and maintain a consistent brand image.

Moreover, Swift's social media influence extends beyond her own career. Her authentic and engaging approach to social media has set a precedent for other artists, demonstrating the power of social media as a tool for connecting with fans and building a loyal following.

Swift's social media presence has also had a significant impact on her fans. Her regular interactions with fans on these platforms have fostered a sense of community among her followers, making them feel seen and valued. This level of engagement has deepened her fans' connection to her and her music.

In conclusion, Swift's social media presence has had a far-reaching influence. It has played a crucial role in her success, shaped the way artists use social media, and fostered a deep sense of connection between Swift and her fans.

C. Her engagement with fans on social media

Taylor Swift's engagement with her fans on social media is a masterclass in community management. She understands the importance of meeting her fans where they are and uses each platform to its full potential to connect with her audience.

Swift's engagement with her fans is not limited to promoting her music and brand. She often interacts with her fans directly, responding to their comments, reblogging their posts, and even surprising them with gifts. This level of engagement has earned her an even higher level of respect from her fans, strengthening their connection with her.

Swift's social media engagement extends beyond individual interactions. She often involves her fans in a social media guessing game, creating anticipation and excitement around her new releases. This interactive approach not only keeps her fans engaged but also creates a sense of community among them.

Swift's engagement with her fans on social media is a testament to her understanding of the digital landscape and her commitment to her fans. It has played a crucial role in her success, helping her to maintain a strong and loyal fanbase.

XIV. THE EVOLUTION OF TAYLOR SWIFT

A. The release of "Lover" and embracing a more positive outlook

The release of Taylor Swift's seventh studio album, "Lover," marked a significant shift in her music and public persona. Following the darker tones of her previous album, "Reputation," "Lover" saw Swift embracing a more positive and romantic outlook.

"Lover" is often described as a reassuringly strong return to Swift's pop roots, with a brighter and more romantic tone than her previous work. The album is filled with songs about love in its various forms, reflecting a more positive and content phase in Swift's life.

The release of "Lover" was also significant in the context of Swift's career. It was her first album released under her new record label, Republic Records, following her departure from Big Machine Records. This move gave Swift more control over her music, allowing her to express herself more freely and authentically.

"Lover" was well-received by fans and critics alike, with many praising its upbeat and romantic sound. The album's positive tone and message of love and acceptance resonated with listeners, further solidifying Swift's status as a pop icon.

In conclusion, the release of "Lover" marked a pivotal moment in Swift's career, showcasing her ability to evolve as an artist and express her personal growth through her music. It is a testament to Swift's resilience and her commitment to staying true to herself, even in the face of adversity.

B. Exploring different genres and artistic styles

Taylor Swift's musical journey is a testament to her versatility as an artist. Known for her ability to seamlessly transition between genres, Swift has explored a range of musical styles throughout her career, continually reinventing her sound while maintaining her unique voice as a songwriter.

Swift's early work was deeply rooted in country music, with her debut album showcasing her storytelling abilities and her knack for crafting catchy, relatable songs. However, as her career progressed, Swift began to experiment with different genres. Her second album, "Fearless," marked her first foray into pop music, a shift that was met with commercial success and critical acclaim.

Swift's musical evolution didn't stop there. Over the years, she has dabbled in various genres, from the synth-pop sounds of "1989" to the indie folk and alternative rock influences of "folklore" and "evermore." Most recently, her album "Lover" saw her exploring a more upbeat and romantic sound, further demonstrating her versatility as an artist.

Swift's ability to explore different genres and artistic styles has not only kept her music fresh and exciting but has also allowed her to reach a broader audience. It's a testament to her creativity and her willingness to push boundaries, further solidifying her status as one of the most influential artists of her generation.

C. The role of personal growth and self-discovery in her journey

The role of personal growth and self-discovery has been a driving force throughout Taylor Swift's remarkable journey in the music industry. As she navigated the complexities of fame, relationships, and artistic evolution, Taylor's commitment to self-discovery became a guiding principle that influenced her music, creativity, and outlook on life.

Taylor's music has always been a reflection of her personal experiences, emotions, and growth. With each album, listeners have been granted an intimate glimpse into her journey of self-discovery. From the innocence of her early country albums to the vulnerability of her more recent releases, Taylor has fearlessly shared her evolving perspectives and emotions with her audience.

Over the years, Taylor's commitment to personal growth and self-discovery has led her to embrace new challenges and take bold creative risks. Her willingness to reinvent her sound and experiment with different musical genres demonstrates her capacity for artistic evolution. This process of exploration has not only kept her music fresh and exciting but has also showcased her fearlessness in embracing change.

Self-discovery has also played a pivotal role in Taylor's journey of empowerment and self-empowerment. As she navigated public scrutiny, media narratives, and societal expectations, Taylor recognized the importance of finding her own voice and asserting her agency. Through her music, she has empowered herself and her listeners to embrace authenticity, self-acceptance, and resilience.

Beyond her music, Taylor's commitment to personal growth has been evident in her philanthropic efforts and advocacy for various causes. Her involvement in charitable organizations and her willingness to use her platform to address social issues reflect her dedication to making a positive impact on the world and leaving a meaningful legacy.

In conclusion, the role of personal growth and self-discovery has been an integral part of Taylor Swift's journey in the music industry. Her commitment to evolving as an artist, embracing change, and using her voice to inspire and empower others serves as a testament to her authenticity and strength. Taylor's journey of self-discovery continues to shape her music, her impact on pop culture, and her influence on fans around the world.

XVI. LEGACY AND IMPACT

A. Taylor Swift's influence
on the music industry

Taylor Swift's influence on the music industry is both profound and multifaceted. She has transformed the music landscape with her storytelling approach to songwriting, pioneering an era of narrative-driven pop music. Her passion for songwriting has inspired a generation of songwriters, as noted by fellow artist Conan Gray.

Swift is also known for her advocacy for artists' rights. She has been vocal about the issues she and other artists face in the music industry, using her platform to push for change. This advocacy extends to her decision to re-record her old albums, a move that has the potential to empower other artists to negotiate better terms with record labels.

Furthermore, Swift's ability to transition seamlessly between musical genres, from country to pop to indie, has demonstrated her versatility as an artist and has had a significant impact on the industry. Her success across different genres has paved the way for other artists to explore genre fluidity.

In addition, Swift's use of social media and her relationship with her fans have reshaped the industry's approach to fan engagement and marketing. Her ability to create anticipation and excitement around her new releases through social media has set a new standard for artist-fan interaction.

In conclusion, Taylor Swift's influence on the music industry is undeniable. From her songwriting and advocacy to her genre fluidity and fan engagement strategies, Swift has left an indelible mark on the industry.

B. The lasting effect on pop culture and future generations

Taylor Swift's impact on pop culture and future generations is nothing short of profound, leaving an enduring legacy that has transcended music and resonated across multiple generations. Through her music, authenticity, and cultural contributions, Taylor has shaped the cultural landscape in ways that will continue to influence artists and fans for years to come.

Taylor's music has become a cultural touchstone, with her albums serving as soundtracks to pivotal moments in the lives of millions. Her ability to capture universal emotions and experiences has made her music relatable to people of all ages, forging a connection that transcends generational boundaries. As a result, her songs continue to be cherished by both longtime fans and new listeners discovering her work.

Beyond her music, Taylor Swift's influence on pop culture extends to her impact on fashion, aesthetics, and social media engagement. Her signature style and red carpet looks have inspired fashion trends and influenced the way fans express themselves through clothing. Additionally, Taylor's use of social media to connect with her audience has set a precedent for artists' engagement with fans in the digital age.

Taylor's resilience and authenticity in the face of media scrutiny and public opinion have set an example for how artists can navigate the challenges of fame while staying true to themselves. Her openness about personal struggles and triumphs has helped destigmatize conversations around mental health, body image, and self-acceptance, leaving a positive impact on both her fans and society at large.

As Taylor Swift continues to evolve as an artist, her influence on future generations remains steadfast. Young artists and aspiring musicians look to her journey as a testament to the power of determination, authenticity, and creative exploration. Her ability to adapt and innovate while staying true to her identity serves as a source of inspiration for those seeking to carve their own paths in the music industry.

In conclusion, Taylor Swift's lasting effect on pop culture and future generations is immeasurable. Her music, authenticity, and cultural contributions have left an indelible mark that will continue to shape the artistic landscape and inspire generations of creators and fans alike. As Taylor's impact continues to ripple through time, her legacy as a trailblazing artist and cultural icon will remain an enduring source of inspiration and admiration.

C. Nurturing new talent and paying it forward

Taylor Swift has consistently demonstrated a commitment to nurturing new talent and paying it forward within the music industry. Recognizing the challenges that aspiring artists often face, she has used her influence and resources to help pave the way for the next generation of musicians, offering support, guidance, and mentorship.

One way Swift has helped nurture new talent is by actively promoting and collaborating with emerging artists. Throughout her career, she has invited lesser-known musicians to join her on stage during her tours, providing them with a platform to showcase their skills to a larger audience. By doing so, she has helped jumpstart the careers of several artists who have gone on to achieve their own success.

Swift has also been known to share advice and guidance with up-and-coming artists, both publicly and privately. She often uses interviews and social media to share tips for aspiring musicians, discussing the importance of perseverance, self-belief, and staying true to oneself. Additionally, she has provided one-on-one mentorship to several new artists, offering personalized advice and support as they navigate the music industry.

In her capacity as a songwriter, Swift has also helped nurture new talent by co-writing songs with emerging artists and songwriters. This not only provides them with the opportunity to learn from her expertise but also helps to elevate their work and expose them to a wider audience.

Swift's philanthropy extends to her support for music education and the arts. She has donated significant amounts of money to schools and organizations focused on music and arts education, ensuring that aspiring musicians have access to the resources they need to develop their skills and pursue their dreams.

Moreover, Swift has advocated for a more equitable and supportive environment within the music industry, championing the rights of all artists and pushing for fair compensation and treatment. This has a broader impact on the industry as a whole, helping to create a more level playing field for new talent.

In summary, Taylor Swift's dedication to nurturing new talent and paying it forward has had a profound impact on the music industry. By actively supporting and mentoring emerging artists, promoting music education, and advocating for a more equitable environment, she has played a significant role in shaping the future of the industry and empowering the next generation of musicians to succeed.

D. Taylor Swift as a symbol of perseverance and resilience

Taylor Swift's journey in the music industry has made her a symbol of perseverance and resilience. From the early stages of her career, she has faced numerous challenges, including public scrutiny, media criticism, and legal battles over her music rights. Yet, through it all, Swift has remained steadfast, continually evolving as an artist and using her experiences to fuel her music.

Swift's resilience is perhaps most evident in her decision to re-record her old albums following a dispute over her music rights. This move, which required a significant amount of time and effort, demonstrated her determination to maintain control over her work. It also sent a powerful message to the music industry about the importance of artists' rights.

Swift's perseverance is also reflected in her music. Many of her songs touch on themes of overcoming adversity and staying true to oneself. These songs have resonated with her fans, many of whom see Swift as a source of inspiration and strength.

In conclusion, Taylor Swift's journey has made her a symbol of perseverance and resilience. Her ability to overcome adversity and stand up for what she believes in has not only shaped her career but has also inspired countless others to do the same.

XVII. VENTURES BEYOND MUSIC

A. Acting career and guest appearances in TV and film

In addition to her illustrious music career, Taylor Swift has also ventured into the world of acting and made guest appearances in TV shows and films. Though her primary focus remains on her music, these roles have allowed her to showcase her versatility and expand her presence in the entertainment industry.

Swift made her acting debut in 2009 with a guest appearance on the popular crime drama series "CSI: Crime Scene Investigation," where she played the role of a rebellious teenager named Haley Jones. This first foray into acting demonstrated her willingness to explore new opportunities and challenge herself creatively.

In 2010, Swift continued to expand her acting resume with a small role in the romantic comedy film "Valentine's Day," directed by Garry Marshall. In the ensemble cast, she played the character Felicia Miller, alongside notable actors such as Jessica Alba, Bradley Cooper, and Anne Hathaway. Her role in the film allowed her to showcase her comedic timing and charm on the big screen.

Swift has also lent her voice to animated films, most notably playing the role of Audrey in the 2012 film "The Lorax," based on the Dr. Seuss book of the same name. Her involvement in the project not only demonstrated her voice acting abilities but also her commitment to environmental conservation, a theme central to the story.

In addition to her film roles, Swift has made guest appearances on various TV shows, such as "New Girl" and "Saturday Night Live." Her appearances on these shows have allowed her to exhibit her comedic skills and engage with her fans in a different capacity. She has also hosted and performed as the musical guest on "Saturday Night Live," further showcasing her versatility as an entertainer.

While Taylor Swift's acting career has not been as extensive as her musical accomplishments, her forays into TV and film have demonstrated her wide-ranging talents and interests. These roles have given her the opportunity to connect with her fans in new ways, explore different facets of her creativity, and leave her mark on the broader entertainment industry.

B. Collaborations with other artists and songwriting for others

Taylor Swift's collaborations with other artists and her songwriting for others have been a significant part of her career, showcasing her versatility and talent as a songwriter.

Swift has collaborated with a number of artists throughout her career. These collaborations often result in unique and memorable songs that blend Swift's songwriting style with the distinctive qualities of her collaborators. Some of her notable collaborations include songs with Ed Sheeran, Bon Iver, and Brendon Urie.

In addition to her collaborations, Swift has also written songs for other artists. For example, she wrote "Best Days of Your Life" for country artist Kellie Pickler. These songwriting ventures highlight Swift's ability to craft songs that cater to the style and voice of other artists, further demonstrating her skill and versatility as a songwriter.

Swift's collaborations and songwriting for others have not only enriched her own discography but have also contributed to the music industry at large. They showcase her ability to work with a variety of artists and genres, and they highlight her significant influence as a songwriter.

Throughout her illustrious career, Taylor Swift has demonstrated her versatility and immense talent not only as a singer and performer but also as a songwriter and collaborator. She has worked with various artists across different genres and has penned songs for other musicians, showcasing her wide-ranging skills and establishing herself as a sought-after creative partner in the music industry.

High-profile collaborations: Taylor Swift has collaborated with a diverse range of artists, including Ed Sheeran, Kendrick Lamar, Gary Lightbody of Snow Patrol, and Bon Iver, among others. These collaborations have resulted in memorable songs that highlight her ability to create unique and engaging music across different genres.

Genre-defying partnerships: Swift's collaborations often showcase her willingness to experiment and push the boundaries of her own musical style. By working with artists from various genres, such as hip-hop, indie, and electronic music, she has expanded her artistic horizons and continued to evolve as a musician.

Co-writing and songwriting for others: In addition to her own music, Swift has lent her songwriting talents to other artists, writing or co-writing tracks for musicians like Calvin Harris, Little Big Town, and Sugarland. These songs not only demonstrate her versatility as a songwriter but also showcase her ability to craft compelling stories and melodies that resonate with a wide range of audiences.

Creative chemistry and mutual respect: Swift's collaborations with other artists are often marked by a strong sense of creative chemistry and mutual respect. She has spoken openly about her admiration for her collaborators and the excitement of working with fellow musicians who inspire her. This collaborative spirit has led to the creation of some of her most memorable and critically acclaimed tracks.

Uncredited contributions: Swift has also been known to contribute to other artists' projects under pseudonyms, such as her work on Calvin Harris's hit song "This Is What You Came For," where she initially used the alias Nils Sjöberg. These uncredited contributions further illustrate her passion for songwriting and her desire to explore her craft in various contexts.

Mentorship and support: Swift's collaborations with other artists often extend beyond the creative process, as she has been known to mentor and support emerging talent in the industry. Her willingness to share her knowledge and experience with others has helped foster a sense of community among musicians and has contributed to the success of many up-and-coming artists.

Taylor Swift's collaborations with other artists and her songwriting for others have played a significant role in shaping her career and enhancing her reputation as a versatile, talented, and generous musician. Her ability to create compelling music across genres and her commitment to supporting and nurturing fellow artists have solidified her status as a true creative force in the music industry.

C. Entrepreneurial pursuits, including her fashion line and fragrance collection

Beyond her achievements in music and acting, Taylor Swift has also ventured into the world of entrepreneurship, using her personal brand and business acumen to create successful ventures in fashion and fragrance. By diversifying her portfolio, Swift has continued to build upon her already impressive career and expand her influence in the entertainment and lifestyle industries.

One of Swift's notable entrepreneurial pursuits has been her foray into the world of fashion. In collaboration with various designers and brands, she has released limited-edition clothing lines that often coincide with her album releases or tours. These collections typically feature a mix of apparel and accessories inspired by her music, personal style, and iconic looks from her music videos. By creating these fashion lines, Swift has provided her fans with an opportunity to express their connection to her music and style, while also capitalizing on her immense popularity and influence in the fashion world.

Swift has also made a significant impact in the fragrance industry with the launch of her own line of perfumes. Her first fragrance, "Wonderstruck," was released in 2011, followed by several other successful fragrances, such as "Wonderstruck Enchanted," "Taylor by Taylor Swift," and "Incredible Things." Each fragrance is uniquely crafted to reflect different aspects of her personality, style, and music, offering fans an intimate connection to their favorite artist. Swift's fragrances have garnered both commercial success and critical acclaim, with her scents often praised for their creativity and appeal to a wide audience.

In addition to her fashion and fragrance ventures, Swift has also explored other entrepreneurial opportunities, such as partnerships with major brands for endorsements and collaborations. These partnerships have allowed her to further expand her brand and reach, while also generating additional revenue streams.

Taylor Swift's entrepreneurial pursuits have not only contributed to her overall success and brand expansion but have also served as an example to other artists looking to diversify their careers. By leveraging her personal brand and business acumen, Swift has solidified her position as a multifaceted icon in the entertainment and lifestyle industries, proving that her talents and influence extend far beyond the realm of music.

XVIII. TAYLOR SWIFT'S INFLUENCE ON ASPIRING MUSICIANS

A. The impact of her journey on aspiring artists

The impact of Taylor Swift's journey on aspiring artists is immeasurable, as her path to success serves as a beacon of inspiration and a roadmap for those looking to make their mark in the music industry. Taylor's story is a testament to the power of determination, authenticity, and resilience, offering valuable lessons and insights for artists navigating their own creative journeys.

Taylor's rise from a young aspiring artist to a global superstar showcases the possibilities that exist for those who are willing to pursue their dreams relentlessly. Her journey serves as a reminder that success often requires perseverance, hard work, and the willingness to overcome obstacles. Aspiring artists can draw inspiration from her early struggles, recognizing that challenges are an integral part of the journey toward achieving their goals.

Moreover, Taylor Swift's dedication to authenticity has resonated deeply with fans and aspiring artists alike. Her openness about her experiences, emotions, and personal growth has fostered a genuine connection with her audience. Aspiring artists can learn from Taylor's commitment to staying true to themselves and their artistry, even in the face of public scrutiny and criticism.

Taylor's approach to songwriting has also left a significant impact on aspiring artists. Her ability to craft relatable and heartfelt lyrics has inspired countless songwriters to delve into their own emotions and experiences. Aspiring artists can draw inspiration from Taylor's storytelling techniques, learning how to infuse their music with sincerity and depth.

Furthermore, Taylor Swift's journey highlights the importance of using one's platform for positive change and making a meaningful impact. Aspiring artists can learn from her advocacy for important causes and her efforts to create a positive influence on society. Taylor's philanthropic endeavors demonstrate that artists have the potential to use their influence to make a difference in the world.

In conclusion, Taylor Swift's journey has had a profound impact on aspiring artists, offering them a source of inspiration, guidance, and encouragement. Her path to success, marked by authenticity, resilience, and artistic growth, serves as a source of motivation for those who aspire to make their mark in the music industry. Aspiring artists can learn from Taylor's experiences and use her story as a source of strength as they navigate their own creative endeavors.

B. Tips and advice from Taylor Swift for those pursuing a career in music

Over the years, Taylor Swift has shared valuable insights and advice for aspiring musicians based on her own experiences in the music industry. Here are some key tips and guidance from Swift that can be helpful for those looking to build a successful career in music:

Believe in yourself: Self-belief is a crucial aspect of pursuing any dream, especially in the competitive world of music. Taylor Swift has consistently emphasized the importance of believing in your talent and abilities, even when faced with rejection or setbacks.

Be authentic: Swift's music is known for its raw honesty and emotional vulnerability. She encourages aspiring musicians to stay true to themselves and their stories, as authenticity in songwriting and performance can create a deep connection with the audience.

Embrace hard work: A strong work ethic is essential for success in the music industry. Swift advises aspiring artists to be prepared to put in the necessary effort, time, and dedication to hone their craft and continually improve.

Develop a unique voice: In a saturated industry, it is essential to stand out from the crowd. Swift encourages emerging artists to find their unique voice and style that sets them apart from others, helping to carve their niche in the music world.

Be open to learning and growth: Swift has continually evolved as an artist throughout her career, exploring new genres and styles. She advises aspiring musicians to remain open to learning and growth, both personally and professionally, as it can lead to new opportunities and creative breakthroughs.

Build a support system: Having a strong support system is essential for emotional well-being and long-term success. Swift emphasizes the importance of surrounding yourself with people who believe in you, share your vision, and are willing to support you on your journey.

Engage with your fans: Swift is known for her close relationship with her fans, and she encourages aspiring artists to actively engage with their audience, both online and in-person. Building a loyal fanbase and fostering a sense of community among your supporters can be crucial for sustained success.

Stand up for yourself and your rights: Swift's advocacy for artists' rights, such as her fight for ownership of her master recordings, serves as a reminder for aspiring musicians to protect their creative work and advocate for their rights within the industry.

Be resilient in the face of adversity: The music industry can be challenging, and setbacks are inevitable. Swift's journey teaches aspiring artists the importance of resilience and perseverance, even when faced with obstacles or criticism.

Stay true to your vision: While it's essential to be open to learning and growth, Swift also emphasizes the importance of staying true to your artistic vision and not compromising on your values or creative integrity.

By following Taylor Swift's tips and advice, aspiring musicians can better navigate the music industry and work towards building a successful and fulfilling career. Her insights, gleaned from years of experience, can serve as a valuable resource for those seeking to make their mark in the world of music.

C. Examples of successful artists influenced by her work

Taylor Swift's work has influenced many artists across different genres, inspiring them to pursue their dreams and shape their own unique sound. Here are a few examples of successful artists who have cited Swift's influence on their music and careers:

Camila Cabello: The former Fifth Harmony member turned solo artist has often spoken about how Taylor Swift's songwriting and storytelling abilities have impacted her own music. Cabello has also credited Swift with teaching her the importance of vulnerability and authenticity in creating songs that connect with listeners.

Halsey: The pop singer-songwriter has cited Taylor Swift as one of her biggest inspirations, particularly in terms of songwriting. Halsey has expressed admiration for Swift's ability to write relatable and heartfelt songs that resonate with a wide range of audiences.

Shawn Mendes: The Canadian pop singer has mentioned in various interviews that he admires Taylor Swift's work ethic, songwriting skills, and her ability to connect with her fans. Mendes has also been influenced by Swift's ability to evolve and adapt her sound throughout her career.

Kelsea Ballerini: The country-pop singer-songwriter has often discussed the impact of Taylor Swift on her career, crediting Swift's early country albums as a significant influence on her own music. Ballerini has expressed her admiration for Swift's storytelling abilities and the way she has navigated her career.

Olivia Rodrigo: The breakout pop star, known for her hit song "drivers license," has cited Taylor Swift as a significant influence on her music, admiring her songwriting and storytelling talents.

Rodrigo has also mentioned that Swift's vulnerability and raw emotions in her music have inspired her own songwriting.

Conan Gray: The indie-pop singer-songwriter has praised Taylor Swift's songwriting abilities, stating that her music has greatly influenced his own work. Gray has expressed admiration for the way Swift can tell stories through her songs, making them feel personal and relatable.

Niall Horan: The former One Direction member has spoken about the impact of Taylor Swift on his own music, particularly in terms of songwriting. Horan has praised Swift's ability to tell stories through her music, which has inspired him to focus on storytelling in his own songwriting.

These are just a few examples of successful artists who have been influenced by Taylor Swift's work. Her impact spans across various genres, inspiring musicians with her songwriting prowess, emotional vulnerability, and the way she has managed her career. Swift's influence on the music industry is undeniable, and her work will likely continue to inspire future generations of artists.

D. The importance of mentorship and support in the music industry

Mentorship plays a crucial role in the music industry. Having a mentor can provide guidance, open doors to opportunities, and expand one's professional network, among other benefits. A good mentor can provide invaluable advice, share their experiences, and help navigate the often complex landscape of the music industry.

Mentors can transform careers by providing insights and advice that can influence decisions, choices, and career trajectory significantly. They can also provide emotional support and encouragement, which can be particularly important in an industry known for its highs and lows.

In addition to mentorship, support from peers and industry professionals is also vital. This support can come in many forms, from collaborations and partnerships to simply providing a listening ear during challenging times. The music industry is a community, and having a strong support system can make all the difference in an artist's career.

In conclusion, mentorship and support are essential in the music industry. They can provide guidance, open doors to opportunities, and offer much-needed support, making them invaluable for any artist's career.

XIX. THE FUTURE OF TAYLOR SWIFT

A. Her plans for future music and tours

Taylor Swift's future in music continues to be a dynamic journey. As of now, she is back on the road with her Eras Tour, her first trek in five years. The tour is a 52-stop U.S. road trip, and she plans to announce international dates in the future. This tour is a testament to her enduring popularity and her commitment to her fans.

In terms of future music, while specific details are often kept under wraps until the right moment, Swift has a history of surprising her fans with new releases. Given her recent activity in re-recording her old albums, it's likely that she will continue to produce new versions of her earlier songs.

Swift's future plans are eagerly anticipated by fans and industry insiders alike. Her ability to continually reinvent herself and her music means that whatever comes next is sure to be exciting. Whether it's new music, tours, or other projects, Taylor Swift's future in the music industry looks bright.

B. Potential new directions
in her career

As an artist known for her ability to reinvent herself, Taylor Swift's career could take many potential new directions. Given her recent foray into indie and alternative music with the albums "folklore" and "evermore," it's possible that Swift might continue to explore these or other new genres in her future work.

Swift's decision to re-record her old albums also opens up new possibilities. She could decide to reinterpret her songs in new ways, giving them a fresh sound while preserving their original spirit. This could also lead to new collaborations with other artists, as she revisits her past work.

Swift's career has also extended beyond music, with ventures into acting and fashion. It's possible that she might choose to further explore these areas in the future. Given her creativity and drive, any new direction she chooses is sure to be met with anticipation and excitement.

In conclusion, while it's impossible to predict exactly what the future holds for Taylor Swift, it's clear that she has many potential new directions to explore in her career. Whatever path she chooses, her fans and the music industry will be eagerly awaiting her next move.

C. Her aspirations outside of music

While Taylor Swift's primary focus has been her music career, she has also shown interest in various other fields. Swift has ventured into acting, with roles in films like "Valentine's Day" and "The Giver," and she has expressed interest in continuing to explore opportunities in film and television.

In addition to acting, Swift has also shown a keen interest in philanthropy. She has been involved in numerous charitable causes over the years, from disaster relief efforts to education initiatives. Swift's philanthropic work demonstrates her commitment to using her platform to make a positive impact on the world.

Swift has also ventured into the world of fashion, launching her own clothing line in collaboration with designer Stella McCartney. This suggests an interest in further exploring the fashion industry.

While it's difficult to predict exactly what Swift's future aspirations might be, it's clear that she has a wide range of interests outside of music. Whether it's acting, philanthropy, fashion, or something entirely new, Swift's future endeavors are sure to be as exciting and impactful as her music career.

XX. CONCLUSION

A. The importance of Taylor Swift's journey as an inspiration to others

The importance of Taylor Swift's journey as an inspiration to others cannot be overstated. Her remarkable story serves as a guiding light for aspiring artists, young individuals, and anyone striving to pursue their dreams with determination, authenticity, and resilience. Taylor's journey embodies the idea that success is not just about talent, but also about the choices we make, the challenges we overcome, and the values we uphold.

Taylor's journey is a testament to the transformative power of passion and dedication. From a young age, she demonstrated an unwavering commitment to her music and a relentless drive to improve her craft. Her meteoric rise from an aspiring artist to a global superstar showcases the incredible possibilities that await those who are willing to work tirelessly to achieve their goals.

Equally significant is Taylor's journey of self-discovery and authenticity. She has been unapologetically herself, openly sharing her experiences, emotions, and personal growth with her audience. By doing so, she has shattered the mold of what a traditional pop star should be and has shown that vulnerability and honesty can be powerful assets in connecting with fans on a profound level.

Taylor's journey also underscores the importance of resilience in the face of adversity. She has navigated the challenges of public scrutiny, media speculation, and personal setbacks with remarkable grace and determination. Her ability to bounce back from setbacks and maintain her focus on her music and creative vision is an invaluable lesson for anyone facing obstacles on their journey.

Moreover, Taylor Swift's journey serves as a reminder that success is not defined solely by achievements, but also by the positive impact one can have on others. Through her philanthropic efforts, advocacy for important causes, and engagement with her fans, Taylor has used her platform to make a meaningful difference in the world. Her actions inspire others to use their influence for good and contribute positively to society.

In conclusion, the importance of Taylor Swift's journey as an inspiration to others is profound. Her story encapsulates the values of determination, authenticity, and resilience, and provides a roadmap for those seeking to pursue their passions and achieve their dreams. Taylor Swift's journey is a beacon of hope that encourages individuals to embrace their uniqueness, overcome challenges, and make a positive impact on the world around them.

B. The power of self-belief and perseverance in achieving success

The power of self-belief and perseverance in achieving success is a central theme in Taylor Swift's journey, serving as a beacon of inspiration for aspiring artists who seek to carve their own paths in the music industry. Taylor's story underscores the importance of believing in oneself, staying true to one's vision, and persisting through challenges to achieve one's dreams.

Taylor Swift's early years were marked by determination and self-belief, even in the face of initial setbacks. Her unwavering confidence in her talent and her refusal to give up propelled her forward. Aspiring artists can learn from Taylor's example, recognizing that self-belief is a driving force that fuels creativity and resilience.

Throughout her career, Taylor's journey has been punctuated by moments of adversity and criticism. Yet, her ability to persevere in the face of challenges has been instrumental in her success. She has shown that setbacks are opportunities for growth and learning, and that the path to success is rarely without obstacles. Aspiring artists can draw strength from Taylor's ability to navigate adversity, understanding that perseverance is essential on the road to achieving their goals.

Taylor's willingness to take risks and embrace change has also been a key factor in her success. She has demonstrated that adapting to new genres, experimenting with different styles, and evolving as an artist are integral to remaining relevant and pushing creative boundaries. Aspiring artists can be inspired by Taylor's openness to change, recognizing that growth and exploration are essential components of artistic development.

Moreover, Taylor Swift's journey highlights the importance of staying true to one's authenticity and artistic vision. She has shown that authenticity resonates with audiences and creates a genuine connection. Aspiring artists can learn from Taylor's commitment to expressing their unique voices and sharing their personal stories through their music.

In conclusion, the power of self-belief and perseverance in achieving success is a central theme in Taylor Swift's journey. Aspiring artists can draw inspiration from her unwavering confidence, resilience in the face of challenges, and commitment to authenticity. Taylor's story serves as a testament to the transformative impact of self-belief and perseverance on the path to realizing one's artistic dreams.

C. Taylor Swift's enduring success and her lasting impact on the world

Taylor Swift's enduring success and her lasting impact on the world are a testament to her exceptional talent, dedication, and ability to connect with audiences on a global scale. Her journey from a young, aspiring artist to a household name has left an indelible mark on the music industry and beyond, shaping the cultural landscape and inspiring generations of fans and aspiring artists alike.

Taylor's ability to evolve and adapt while staying true to her artistic vision has been a key factor in her enduring success. Her music has transcended genres, resonating with listeners of all ages and backgrounds. Her albums, from the country-infused beginnings to the bold pop anthems, have consistently topped charts and captured the hearts of millions.

Beyond her chart-topping hits, Taylor's impact extends to the way she has redefined the relationship between artists and their fans. Her personal interactions with fans, genuine appreciation for their support, and engagement on social media have fostered a deep and lasting connection. This unique bond has contributed to the longevity of her success and her influence on pop culture.

Taylor Swift's legacy also lies in her role as a trailblazer for women in the music industry. She has broken down barriers, challenged stereotypes, and championed gender equality. Her advocacy for artists' rights and her efforts to empower women have reshaped the narrative of female artists' place in the industry, leaving an impact that will be felt for years to come.

Furthermore, Taylor's philanthropic endeavors have demonstrated her commitment to making a positive impact on the world. From supporting education initiatives to aiding disaster relief efforts, she has used her influence and resources to effect change and improve the lives of others. Her dedication to giving back underscores her role as a role model and source of inspiration.

Taylor Swift's enduring success is a result of her ability to connect deeply with her audience by speaking to universal emotions and experiences. Her lyrics are relatable and her music evokes feelings that resonate across cultures and generations. This universality has solidified her position as an artist whose influence will continue to transcend time.

In conclusion, Taylor Swift's enduring success and lasting impact on the world are a testament to her remarkable journey and the profound connections she has forged with her audience. Her ability to evolve, connect, and use her platform for positive change has solidified her as not only a musical icon, but also a cultural force whose legacy will continue to shape the world for years to come.

A SkyCuration
★★★★★

Made in the USA
Las Vegas, NV
18 October 2023

79324663R00069